zr

DATE DUE

SEP 1 0 1996 106	107	MAY 1 6 1997
SEP 1 3 1996	101	SEP 2 5 1997
SEP 2 3 1996 108	109	OCT 7 1997
SEP 3 0 1996 110	106	OCT 2 7 1997
OCT 9 1996 105	106	NOV 1 0 1997
NOV 1 4 1996 K-103	Kom	JAN 1 3 1998
NOV 2 1 1996 K 103	108	JAN 3 9 1998
DEC 1 6 1996 110	114	MAY 2 8 1998
JAN 1 3 1997 5	56	JUL 2 8 1998
JAN 2 7 1997 110	SEP 09	SEP 2 1 1999
JAN 2 3 1997 K-103		
MAY 1 5 1997 K-103		

Powerboat Racing

Jay H. Smith

Reading consultant:
John Manning, Professor of Reading
University of Minnesota

Illustrated with photographs
by Jim Vota

Capstone Press

MINNEAPOLIS

Printed in the United States of America.

Capstone Press • 2440 Fernbrook Lane • Minneapolis, MN 55447

Editorial Director   John Coughlan
Managing Editor   John Martin
Copy Editor   Gil Chandler

Library of Congress Cataloging-in-Publication Data

Smith, Jay H.
    Powerboat racing / by Jay H. Smith.
        p. cm.   (Motorsports)
    Includes bibliographical references and index.
    ISBN 1-56065-231-4
    1. Motorboat racing--Juvenile literature. [1. Motorboat
    racing.]   I. Title.   II. Series.
    GV835.9.S65   1995
    797.1'25--dc20   94-22626
                                                               CIP
                                                               AC

ISBN: 1-56065-231-4

99 98 97 96 95   8 7 6 5 4 3 2 1

Table of Contents

Chapter 1
Powerboat Racing

There are many different kinds of races, and many different racing vehicles. There are also many kinds of race tracks. Indy cars and stock cars speed around oval tracks. Dragsters zip down a narrow strip of asphalt. Bicyclists follow public roads and highways, and motocross riders tumble over rough and rocky hills.

The powerboat racer has a special challenge–a track made of water. The course, marked by floating buoys, runs a few hundred yards offshore. Wind and waves push the speeding

boats to and fro, making high-speed competition tricky and very dangerous.

Many powerboat racers have suffered accidents and even death in competition. Yet the sport continues to grow in popularity. Fans love the speed and excitement. Drivers are eager to

test their skill and courage. Boat designers build faster, bigger, more powerful craft. Sponsors pour millions of dollars into their racing teams. There's nothing quite like the thrill of powerboat racing!

Chapter 2

Speed on Water

In the 1800s, the French invented the sport of automobile racing. They also invented boat racing.

The French put car engines on boats. The first international motorboat races were held in 1898, on the Seine River in Paris, France. At that race, the winning boat was clocked at 15 miles (24.1 kilometers) per hour. That speed may seem slow today. In 1898 it was fast enough to beat the competition.

Motorboating in Europe

By 1904, the motorboat craze had caught on throughout Europe. At one race that year, the winner was clocked at 25 miles (40.25 kilometers) per hour.

European car companies entered boats in races. Their engines were fueled by gasoline and a cheap kind of oil.

The boats were getting faster, but they weren't getting any safer. The 1904 race was

full of accidents. When a boat caught fire, the crew had to jump into the water.

Motorboating in North America

Many Americans became interested in motorboat racing. By 1903, races were being held off the shore of New Jersey.

To make the races fair, rules were needed. In 1903 the American Power Boat Association (APBA) was formed to set down guidelines for the new sport.

This historic powerboat is made of mahogany, a hard and durable wood.

Powerboating is Born

By the summer of 1904, the American Power Boat Association was sponsoring dozens of races. These organized races were held at yacht clubs across the United States.

Some boats were always faster than others. To make the races more competitive, the American Power Boat Association began to divide boats into classes. Racers would compete only against others with similar boats.

Powerboating's First Superstar

In the 1920s, an American named Gar Wood became the sport's first superstar. Wood's high-powered boats were almost unbeatable. In fact, only one person showed up to challenge Wood for the 1921 Gold Cup, the world championship of powerboating.

The American Power Boat Association soon began to worry that Wood was winning too easily. They passed a rule limiting the power of boats in Gold Cup races. In 1922, 13 boats entered the race. The fastest barely reached 40 miles (64.4 kilometers) per hour. That was only half Wood's winning speed in 1920.

Wood continued to dominate international races. In 1931, he became the first powerboat driver to break 100 miles (160 kilometers) per hour. In 1932, he set a world record of 124.9 (201 kilometers) per hour.

Chapter 3
Today's Boats

Powerboats have come a long way from the heavy, wooden craft of the early years. New materials and new designs have made the modern powerboat a marvel of engineering.

The powerful engines and lightweight hulls of these boats allow them to travel at incredible speeds.

The Hulls

The hulls of today's powerboats can be made of wood, metal, or lightweight **fiberglass**. Because fiberglass is lighter than

A hydroplane idles before the start of a race.

either wood or metal, it's the most common
material used by boat designers. The weight,
length, width, and shape of the hull all affect
how a boat handles.

Deep-V's

One type of powerboat hull is called the **V-
bottom**. As the name suggests, a V-bottom is

shaped like a letter "V." The most common of these hulls is called the **deep-V**. The deep-V's design allows it to stay on course with little steering. But the shape of a deep-V makes it difficult to steer around corners.

Hydroplanes

Another hull design is the **hydroplane**. The first hydroplane was the British-built *Pioneer*, built in 1910. Hydroplane hulls are usually built of lightweight **aluminum**.

Pontoons called **sponsons** are added to each side of a hydroplane's hull. These help prevent the hydroplane from tipping at high speeds.

As the hydroplane speeds along, only the sponsons and **propeller**, or **prop**, touch the water. And these parts *barely* touch the water. Most of the boat is actually in the air. It glides above the surface like an airplane. That's how the hydroplane got its name.

Hydroplanes cut through the air at high speeds, with only their back ends touching the water.

In the early hydroplanes, the driver sat in the back. The engine was mounted in front. Today, the **cabover** design is the most popular type of hydroplane. In a cabover, the driver sits in the middle of the boat. The engine is behind him. If the engine should catch fire, the driver is protected from the flames. The cabover design makes the hydroplane safer and easier to steer.

Powerboat engines are complex machines that need careful maintenance.

The Catamaran

A third type of hull is the **catamaran**. A catamaran has two thin hulls connected by a platform. Both the driver and the engine sit on the platform. Because the catamaran is made of two thin hulls, less of the boat touches the water. This creates less **resistance**. Many drivers feel the catamaran is more difficult to steer because it has two hulls

Less resistance makes the catamaran a very fast boat. Today, catamarans regularly win APBA-sponsored races.

The Engines

What moves these different types of hulls through the water at such great speeds? Powerboat motors, of course. There are many different kinds of racing engines. They vary in size, the type of fuel they use, and how they are attached to the hull.

Inboard or Outboard?

Like the engine of a car, an **inboard motor** can't be seen from outside the boat. Like a car's engine, an inboard isn't meant to be removed. It's part of the boat.

Prop Problems

Powerboats that use inboards may also have more than one engine. If one engine quits, the other can bring the boat to shore for repairs.

Powerboat engines are linked to the propeller, which spins in the water to move the boat forward. But because props on boat

engines cause **drag**, a boat with more than one
engine has extra drag.

    Outboard motors are attached to the boat
after it's built. Outboard motors look much
like the motors on fishing boats. Powerboats
have as many as three outboards attached to the

hull. These racing outboards are big–often too big for a single person to lift.

Props once affected the steering of powerboats. When props spin, they push the boat slightly off to the right or the left. To stay on course, drivers had to steer a little in the opposite direction. Modern boat designers have corrected this problem. By turning the prop on the **starboard**, or right, side in the opposite direction to the prop on the **port** (left) side, the boat stays on a straight course.

The Racing Engine

Many of the powerboats which compete in today's races have inboard engines specially designed by auto makers like Chevrolet or Ford. Many of these engines are actually built for cars or trucks.

Other racing events allow the use of engines which have been modified by the racers.

Chapter 4
Kinds of Racing

The American Power Boat Association **sponsors** races in several categories. The category a racer enters depends on two things. The first is whether the boat has an outboard or inboard engine. The second is the design of the boat's hull.

Unlimited Hydroplanes

In 1946, the American Power Boat Association cancelled the rules against high-powered boats it had made when Gar Wood

The powerful aircraft engines in an Unlimited hydroplane can push the boats to a speed of 200 miles (320 kilometers) per hour.

Unlimiteds are built for speed.

dominated racing. Racers began to fit their
hydroplanes with engines from World War II
fighter planes. These hydroplanes were
allowed unlimited power. These boats, called
Unlimited hydroplanes, were built for speed.

Today, Unlimited hydroplanes are also
known as **Thunderboats.** Thunderboats are
between 24 and 28 feet (7.2 and 8.4 meters)
long. Because they are powered by huge
airplane engines, their drivers must be highly

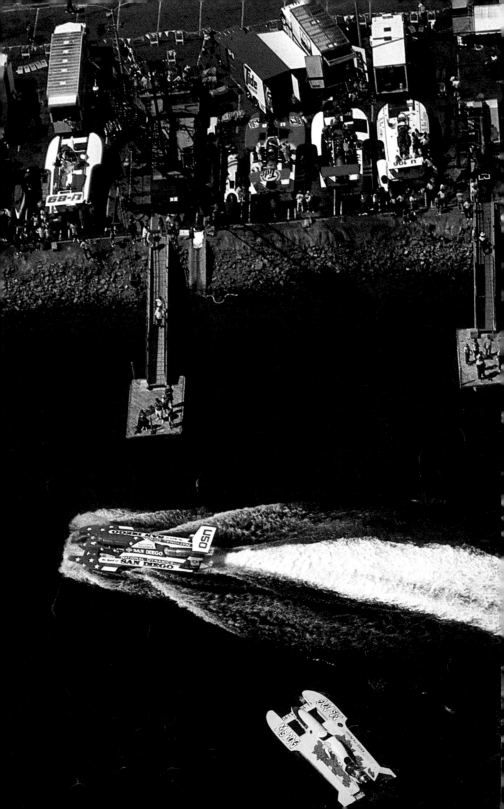

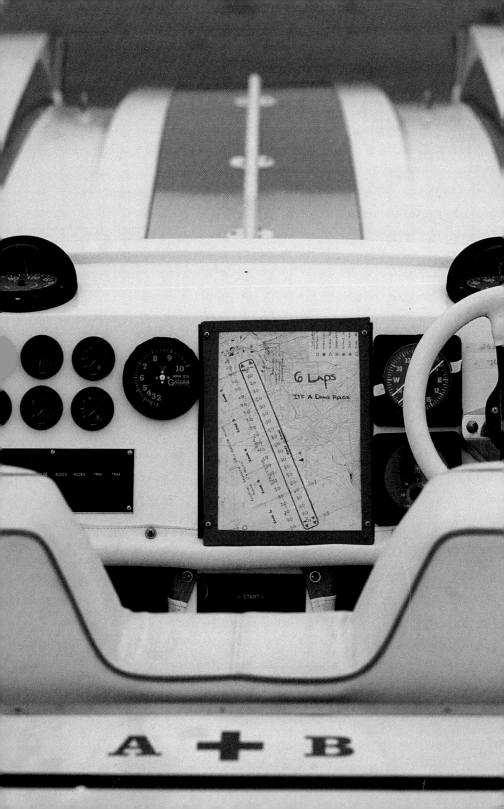

skilled. These drivers race their hydroplanes around an oval course which may vary in length from 1.66 to 2.5 miles (2.66 to 4.0 kilometers). They push their boats to speeds of 200 miles (320 kilometers) per hour.

The Thunderboat racers compete for the APBA Gold Cup, powerboat racing's most famous prize.

Offshore Racing

Offshore racing is a test of teamwork, speed, and endurance. Three-member crews race catamarans or deep-V's which can be as long as 50 feet (15 meters).

The first crew member is the driver. He or she is responsible for steering. The **throttleperson** controls the flow of fuel to the engine. The third crew member is the **navigator**. The navigator uses compasses and maps to keep the boat on course.

The charts and instruments on a powerboat help the crew keep the boat on course and under control.

The course can be anywhere from 100 to 200 miles (160 to 320 kilometers) long. The boats usually have multiple inboard or outboard motors. Crews compete against each other as well as against rough seas and weather.

Drag Racing

Drag-racing boats are the fastest on any water. Like drag-racing cars, they race one-on-one. The course is a quarter-mile (400 meter) **straightaway**. Speeds go as high as 200 miles (320 kilometers) per hour.

Stock Outboard Racing

Stock outboard racing is the ideal competition for beginning racers. Many famous drivers began their careers in this category.

"Stock" means that the engines are used just as they were produced by an outboard factory. Racers may not alter them. Stock outboard racing equipment is inexpensive compared to the equipment used in other types of racing.

This racing category is set up in classes for different engine sizes. Stock outboard boats–either hydroplanes or **runabouts**–reach speeds of 40 to 80 miles (64 to 128 kilometers) per hour.

Modified Outboard Racing

This is the next step for beginning racers who have mastered the stock outboard category. **Modified outboard** racers are allowed to modify, or change, their factory engines to make them faster. These boats, which can be either hydroplanes or runabouts, are pushed to speeds of 60 to 90 miles (96 to 144 kilometers) per hour.

Chapter 5
Racing Safety

In November 1980, Lee Taylor was attempting to break the world speed record. He was racing on Lake Tahoe in Nevada. But when his boat reached 230 miles (368 kilometers) per hour, it exploded. The engine just could not handle the power it created.

In 1981, Bill Muncey, an eight-time Gold Cup winner, was killed in a **blowover**. The powerful current of air lifted and flipped his craft, slamming it back to the surface upside down.

Riding a personal watercraft is a safe way to prepare for the challenge of powerboat racing.

Faster speeds mean greater risks for modern powerboat drivers.

Dean Chenoweth was the second unlimited driver to break the 200-mile (320-kilometer) per-hour mark. In 1982, his boat flipped over and crashed. Chenoweth died instantly.

Three of the world's top powerboat drivers had been killed in a little more than a year. Drivers and the American Power Boat Association began to look again at powerboat racing's safety rules.

Safety Today

No matter how many rules are made for a sport, there will be accidents. Most racing accidents occur in competition.

Today each powerboat racing category has specific safety rules to be followed. Unlimited hydroplanes, for example, must automatically shut down if the driver is thrown from the **cockpit**.

In addition, crew members must wear safety equipment. Helmets and **life preservers** are required. **Fire retardant** suits, gloves, and socks also must be worn.

All boats have fire extinguishers which automatically turn on in case of fires. Paramedics and patrol boats must attend each race.

Powerboat racers have a number of ways to communicate with those on shore in case of an emergency. All boats, for example, are equipped with **strobe lights**. When a driver is in trouble, he or she turns the light on. This tells those on shore that he or she is all right but needs assistance. Drivers also use hand signals to communicate to observers. These signals tell race officials if help is needed.

Every spectator at a powerboat race feels the excitement. The colorful machines and the roar of finely-tuned engines add to the thrill of the race. There's even a chance of seeing a record broken.

The speed and excitement of powerboat racing are sure to make this sport even more popular in the future.

Glossary

aluminum–a lightweight metal

blowover–a powerboat mishap that occurs when air going under the hull causes the boat to fly into the air and flip over

cabover–a powerboat design which situates the cockpit over the center of the craft.

catamaran–a boat with two parallel hulls

cockpit–the part of the powerboat where the driver sits

deep-V–the name for a hull shaped like the letter "V"

drag–something that slows or stops motion

drag race–a race between two powerboats on a straight course to determine which can accelerate faster from a standstill

fiberglass–a material made from glass fibers bonded together with plastic

fire retardant–to have fire-resistant qualities

hydroplane–a motorboat designed to move at high speed with only a small part of its hull touching the water

hull–the framework of a motorboat or ship

inboard motor–an engine mounted inside a boat

life preserver–a device like a belt or jacket designed to keep a person afloat

modified outboard–an outboard engine made faster with special parts

navigator–a crew member who pilots the course of a boat for the driver

offshore racing–racing that takes place on the open ocean

outboard motor–an engine mounted on the outside of a boat

port–facing forward, the left side of a ship

propeller *or* **prop**–a rotary, fan-like device

resistance–a force that opposes or stops motion

sponson–pontoons on the hull of a hydroplane

sponsor–a business that pays in return for advertising

starboard–facing forward, the right side of ship

stock outboard–an outboard motor that is just as made by the manufacturer

straightaway–a straight course

strobe light–a lamp that produces short, intense flashes of light by means of an electric discharge in a gas

throttleperson–the crew member who controls the flow of fuel to the engine

thunderboat–another name for the Unlimited hydroplane

Unlimited hydroplane–the fastest class of hydroplane

V-bottom–the "V"-shaped planing bottom of a boat

To Learn More

Andersen, T. J. *Power Boat Racing*. Mankato, MN: Crestwood House, 1988.

Kentley, Eric. *Boat* (Eyewitness Books). New York: Alfred A. Knopf, 1992.

Some Useful Addresses

American Power Boat Association
17640 E. Nine Mile Road
Eastpointe, MI   48021

Boat Owners Association of the U.S.
880 South Pickett Street
Alexandria, VA   22304

Aquatic Hall of Fame and Museum of Canada
435 Main Street
Winnipeg, MB   R3B 1B2

National Motorsports Hall of Fame
20 Division Street
Coldwater, MI   49038

Motorsports Museum and Hall of Fame
45225 West Ten Mile Road
Nori, MI   48050

Canadian Power and Sail Squadrons
26 Golden Gate Court
Scarborough, ON   M1P 3A5

Index

accidents, 6, 11, 37-39
aluminum, 17
American Power Boat
 Association (APBA),
 11-13, 21, 27, 31, 38
automobile racing, 9

blowovers, 37

cabover design, 19
catamarans, 20, 31
Chenoweth, Dean, 37-
 38
Chevrolet, 25
clothing, 39
crews, 31, 33

designers, 7, 25
drag-racing boats, 33

engines, 9, 15, 19-23,
 25, 27, 31, 33-34, 37,
 40; inboards, 21, 25;
 outboards, 23
Europe, 9-10

fiberglass, 15-16
fire, 11, 19, 39
Ford, 25
fuel, 10

Gold Cup, 13, 31, 37

handling, 16-17, 19-
 21, 25
hulls, 15-23, 27
hydroplanes, 17-19,
 34; Unlimited
 hydroplanes, 27-28,
 37, 39